DREAM JOBS IN SPORTS PERSONNEL

CARLA MOONEY

THE LEAGUE

Rosen
YA™

New York

Published in 2018 by The Rosen Publishing Group, Inc.
29 East 21st Street, New York, NY 10010

First Edition

Library of Congress Cataloging-in-Publication Data

Names: Mooney, Carla, 1970– author.
Title: Dream Jobs in Sports Personnel / Carla Mooney.
Description: New York : Rosen Publishing, 2018. | Series: Great Careers in the Sports Industry | Includes bibliographical references and index. | Audience: Grades 7–12.
Identifiers: LCCN 2017017093 | ISBN 9781538381427 (library bound) | ISBN 9781508178637 (paperback)
Subjects: LCSH: Sports personnel—Juvenile literature. | Sports—Vocational guidance—Juvenile literature.
Classification: LCC GV734.3 .M64 2018 | DDC 796.023—dc23
LC record available at https://lccn.loc.gov/2017017093

Manufactured in China

CONTENTS

Tyreke Evans of the NBA's New Orleans Pelicans plays against the Washington Wizards' Jason Smith during a 2017 game at the Verizon Center in Washington, DC.

In April 2016, the National Basketball Association (NBA) announced that it would become the first major United States sports league to allow corporate logos on player uniforms. Beginning in the 2017–18 season, the ads will be 2.5-inch (6-centimeter) square patches on the left shoulder of players' uniforms. Teams will keep 50 percent of the revenue from the corporate ads, while the other half will go to the NBA's revenue-sharing pool. "Jersey sponsorships provide deeper engagement with partners looking to build a unique association with our teams and the additional investment will help grow the game in exciting new ways," said NBA commissioner Adam Silver in an article posted on CNN .com. "We're always thinking about innovative ways the NBA can remain competitive in a global marketplace, and we are excited to see the results of this three-year trial."

As each team will sell its own ad space to sponsors, the job will fall to people like Sam Cole, the director of corporate partnerships for the NBA's New Orleans Pelicans. In his job, Cole is responsible for developing, enhancing, and renewing corporate relationships. He and his sales team sell sponsorship packages to local, regional, and national companies. They develop presentations and proposals for sponsors and present ideas and opportunities for sponsors to grow their business with the team. Working with other team personnel, they make sure that all contractual requirements of a corporate sponsorship are met, including game day programs, community programs, hospitality, internet and social media promotions, print ads, stadium signage, and television and radio promotions.

Closing a sponsorship deal is a lot of work. "Despite what people think, our phones are not ringing off the hook with companies begging us to take their money. Even the most successful teams/properties don't see that," Cole said in an article posted on WorkInSports .com. He says that putting together a sponsorship deal takes patience and persistence. He's seen many deals fall apart when a sales person gets impatient and pushes too hard or backs off too soon when a corporate partner moves slowly. However, when he closes a sponsorship deal, Cole says the feeling is like no other. "It's definitely an adrenaline rush and is the best motivator to get you going after the next deal," he said in an article posted on WorkInSports.com.

Jobs like Cole's are some of many opportunities to work behind the scenes in the sports industry. Careers in sports personnel may not be in front of the camera or on the field, but they are integral to the success of sports teams, leagues, and organizations around the world. It is a wide career field that includes many type of positions, from accounting and public relations to talent evaluations and human resources. Sports personnel jobs are needed at every level of sports, from high school, through college, and to the professional leagues, both major and minor. Regardless of job function, sports personnel employees help a team or organization manage its daily operations so it can reach its goals and objectives.

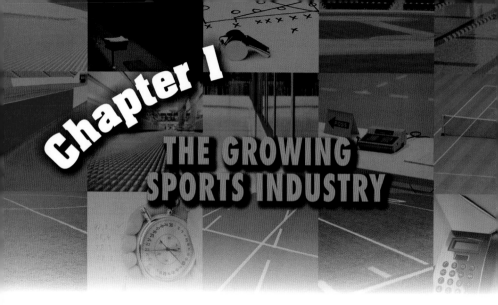

Chapter 1

THE GROWING SPORTS INDUSTRY

Many young athletes who play soccer, football, basketball, baseball, and other sports dream of becoming professional athletes. Realistically, however, only a very small percentage of youth athletes will grow up to have professional sports careers. And those that do make it to the professional leagues often play for only a few short years. For many athletes, injuries or other problems prematurely end their careers. For example, in the National Football League, the average player's career lasts for only 3.3 years. In the National Basketball Association, the average career of a player is not much longer, at only 4.8 years.

While only a select few turn their athletic skills on the field or court into a successful career, there are many other ways to become involved in the sports industry and launch a sports-related career. Sports are a big business, and businesses need people to run them. The sports industry is worth tens of billions of dollars and will

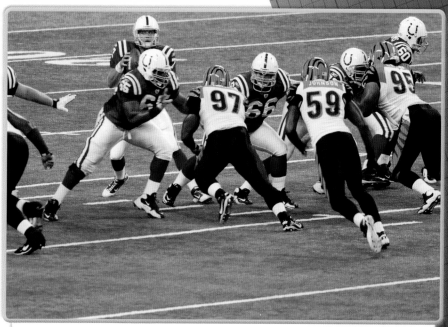

The quarterback drops back and scans the field for an open receiver during a game between the National Football League's Indianapolis Colts and Cincinnati Bengals.

continue to grow over time. The revenue generated by the industry has grown tremendously over the past few decades, driven by the television broadcasting of games. With larger audiences watching games, more companies are buying advertising to get their product and message in front of the audience. And corporate sponsorships and stadium naming rights have emerged as new innovations for marketing in sports. Today, the main revenue drivers for the sports industry are gate revenues, media rights, sponsorships, and merchandising.

THE BIG FOUR

In the United States, the Big Four spectator sports are baseball, basketball, football, and hockey. These sports generate the most fan interest, media attention, and as a result, revenue. Each of these sports has a governing body—Major League Baseball (MLB), the National Basketball Association (NBA), the National Football League (NFL), and the National Hockey League (NHL). At first, these governing bodies operated to create and enforce rules and policies that governed owners, players, and referees. They also organized games between teams, maintained statistics, and issued awards to winning teams and players.

While they still perform these functions, the sports industry's tremendous

(continued on page 12)

Players from the New York Rangers and New Jersey Devils battle in front of the net during a hockey game in Newark, New Jersey.

(continued from page 10)

growth has launched these organizations into fully operating businesses. Today, each of these organizations performs marketing and public relations functions for their league. They also negotiate deals for logo licensing and merchandising, license television rights, and perform revenue distribution among teams in their league.

The MLB, NBA, and NHL also own and operate minor league teams, which operate under their own governing bodies. These minor league teams, along with collegiate and high school teams, often give many sports personnel professionals their first step into the industry.

The sports industry has managed to thrive even when the country's economy stumbles. People living on a budget will often cut back in other areas such as going out to a restaurant or taking a vacation in order to save the money to buy tickets to a sporting event. Industry analysts credit the improvements in broadcasting and technology, the growth of social media, and the increase in sports publications and websites with creating more interest than ever in sports.

In such as large and growing industry, there are many opportunities to work in all areas and all levels of sports, both on and off the field. "Maybe [high school students] have played, maybe they have a passion for sports, a love of sports, and they're wondering, 'how can I stay involved with this?' They might not be playing Division I, but can still be connected," said Brian Smith, assistant dean of Colangelo College of Business at Grand Canyon University in Phoenix and director of the sports business major, in an article in *USA Today*. "This is way more than the game on the floor. There's this huge industry." These jobs support the sports industry by providing coaching and player development, mental and physical health services, sales and marketing, legal and financial services, and sports media content.

CAREERS IN SPORTS PERSONNEL

In sports, athletes on the field are in the public eye. Behind the scenes, an army of people work to manage the day-to-day business of sports. These people work in a team's back offices as legal specialists, accountants, human resources personnel, financial planners, and other positions to manage the business of sports for teams and companies. They work in sales and marketing, selling ticket packages and advertising new promotions to attract fans to the game. They negotiate and work with sponsors, planning promotional events and sponsor advertising. Media specialists and communications employees handle press releases, traditional media, and social media accounts.

Boston Red Sox fans yell as Alex Rodriguez of the rival New York Yankees warms up on deck before batting in a game at Fenway Park in Boston.

Outside of the office, even more people work behind the scenes to put together the teams that fans see competing on the field. Talent scouts identify and recruit players and manage the player development side of sports. Athletic trainers and staff manage the athletes' health and well-being and get them back on the field as quickly as possible after an injury.

MOVING UP IN MAJOR LEAGUE BASEBALL'S SPORTS PERSONNEL

Sometimes, a person's career in the sports industry can take several turns, leading to unexpected places. Alex Anthopoulos is the vice president of baseball operations for the Los Angeles Dodgers.

Growing up in Montreal, Quebec, Anthopoulos graduated from McMaster University in Ontario, Canada, with a degree in economics. He did not immediately pursue a career in sports. In fact, Anthopoulos returned home to Montreal after graduation to take over the family heating and ventilation business after his father's death. After two years, he realized that he wanted to pursue a career in sports. He sent out letters to every Major League Baseball (MLB) team, looking for any sort of job to get his foot in the door. Eventually, the Montreal Expos offered him an unpaid job. He worked in the team's mail room sorting fan mail.

Anthopoulos used that first opportunity as a stepping stone. When a paid position as a media relations assistant opened up with the Expos, he got the job. "The biggest thing I did with the fan mail thing [his unpaid job with the Expos]—and I can't stress this enough—is the importance of humility in anything you do. I walked in, I had a tie, I had a shirt, I dressed right, I sat in the corner, I shut my mouth and my goal was I was going to be the best fan mail guy these guys have ever had or seen," he said in an article posted on WorkInSports.com.

Over the years, Anthopoulos moved into different sports personnel positions, learning different aspects about Major League Baseball in each. He worked as a scouting department in-office coordinator for the Florida Marlins, then moved up to become an area scout for the team. Next, Anthopoulos advanced to become the scouting coordinator for the Toronto Blue Jays, eventually moving into the assistant general manager, vice president of baseball operations, and general manager roles.

As Toronto's general manager, Anthopoulos spends a lot of his time working on contracts with players and other personnel and talking with the scouting department about prospective players. He says that every day is a blur of meetings, nonstop phone calls, emails, text messages, games, workouts, and more texts. "You're going a million miles an hour in this job. A million texts. A million phones calls. You have to talk to everybody about everything. And you know what, if you're in this job, you like the pace," he said in the WorkInSports.com article. One typical day during spring training, Anthopoulos wakes at 4 a.m. He spends a little time with his young family, then heads to a 9 a.m. meeting with his pro scouts, all of them in the same room before they head out to their assignments for the season. "Today we went through the other 29 organizations in baseball," said Anthopoulos. "We want to project to everyone how the next few years are set up. The areas we want to target. The players we want to target. It's an important process to go through."

After the scouting meeting and phone calls with a few player agents, Anthopoulos heads to the minor league camp to observe the precamp the team is running for prospects. Then he heads over to the team's spring training game. He multitasks, switching his attention back and

A woman working behind the scenes in one of the many jobs in sports personnel studies a spreadsheet for information about players.

forth between the team on the field and another ball game on the television in his private box. He notices a player on the television and makes a mental note to ask his scouts about the reports on the player. Meanwhile, the phone continues to ring, and Anthopoulos moves on to the next task.

WITH NUMEROUS OPPORTUNITIES COMES FIERCE COMPETITION

There are numerous opportunities to work in sports behind the scenes in any number of sports personnel roles, from talent evaluators to accountants. "While the number of professional sports teams has stayed largely constant

Students speak with potential employers during a crowded job fair. Because jobs in sports personnel are often highly desired, the competition can be fierce.

over time, the addition of jobs created by the growth of technology—from system engineering, to analytics and social media—has opened up thousands of additional positions that did not exist a decade ago," Jason Betzer, a sports attorney and founder of GAME, Inc., writes in an article for Forbes.com. In addition, the inflow of billions of dollars in television and sponsorship dollars, along with private investments into businesses, has created more opportunities in sports marketing, management, and consulting.

Even so, because these positions are often highly desired, the competition to land a job in the sports industry is often fierce. Betzer recommends that job seekers be open minded about potential careers and learn as much as they can about a career or position. "Be sure to gather as much information as possible—through colleagues, networking contacts, recruiters and research—to ensure a position is worth pursuing, and would take you in the direction you want your career to progress," he writes in the Forbes.com article. As the sports industry continues to grow across all levels, it is an exciting time to pursue a career in sports personnel.

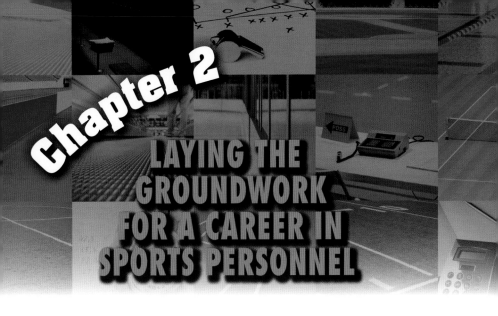

Chapter 2

LAYING THE GROUNDWORK FOR A CAREER IN SPORTS PERSONNEL

Interested in a career in sports personnel? There are several ways that high school students can lay the groundwork for a future career in the sports industry. From working as a referee to taking community college classes, these ideas can help a high school student take the next step toward a career in sports.

PLAY ON SPORTS TEAMS

One of the best ways to prepare for a career in sports is to experience it firsthand. Playing on a sports team teaches students about working together as a team, overcoming adversity, the importance of good practice habits, and sportsmanship. All of these qualities can be applied in a future sports personnel career, no matter what the position is.

A woman works as a referee at an Olympic hockey game. Working as an official or referee at any level can provide valuable firsthand experience for a career in sports.

In addition, playing on a sports team allows a student to make contacts with coaches, trainers, officials, and others in the sports scene. They may become mentors that the student can ask for career advice in the future.

BE A STUDENT MANAGER

Not every kid who is interested in a sports career has the athletic talent to make his or her high school team. If students cannot play on a sports team, they can still get involved in the team by volunteering to be a student manager. Some students may even volunteer to be a student manager for a sport they do not play. For example, a girl who plays on the

A young man prepares to use a bar code scanner on boxes of sports equipment and uniforms that have arrived in a warehouse.

varsity soccer team in the fall may volunteer to be a student manager in the spring for her school's lacrosse team.

Students who have experience being student managers in high school may be able to use that experience to land a position as a college team manager. For some elite athletic programs, a student manager is a highly coveted and competitive position. For example, at the top NCAA (National Collegiate Athletic Association) basketball schools, the athletic staff sifts through hundreds of applications annually, choosing only a handful of student managers each year. The application process can be intense. Some schools, like Michigan State, require candidates to job shadow and write an essay. Kentucky asks applicants to work camp before inviting some for interviews. And applicants at Duke go through multiple rounds of interviews.

Ryan Kelly was invited to become a member of Duke Basketball's student manager staff of twelve when he was a freshman. "I was the happiest kid in the world," Kelly said in an article on ESPN.com. "I was running around the dorm like a nut." That year, he remembers wheeling a tub of Gatorade on a dolly down a hallway in Duke's Cameron Indoor Stadium. When he lost control of the dolly, the orange liquid spilled everywhere, just as Duke basketball coach Mike Krzyzewski turned the corner. "Oh my god. I thought I was going to get fired," Kelly said in the ESPN article. Luckily Coach K just laughed and remarked that Kelly must be a freshman.

FINDING A MENTOR

Finding a mentor can help people achieve their career goals. A mentor is a person who works in the industry and has experience and can give advice to a person just starting out in his or her career. A good mentor can help a high school student evaluate volunteer opportunities and decide what classes to take in school. As the student enters college and beyond, a mentor can offer advice on everything from college classes to dealing with a difficult supervisor. And because mentors often have industry contacts, they may be able to help a student get a job or land an internship.

Finding a good mentor generally happens naturally. Most people do not go up to a stranger and ask the person to be their mentor. Instead, the relationship develops over time. When a student does a good job – either with a sports team, at work, or in a volunteer position—supervisors and other adults will notice. Once a student establishes himself or herself as a serious worker and good performer, he or she can ask a mentor smart questions about the business and industry. Eventually, the conversation can turn toward career questions. When dealing with a mentor, students should always be respectful of the other person's time and not be too demanding. Be patient, and a mentor can be a powerful asset on the way to a career in sports.

Most of the time, the job of a student manager is not glamorous. Managers haul luggage onto planes and buses at all hours of the day and night. They fill and refill Gatorade tubs and cut and edit film. They chart plays and stats at games, work camps in the summer, and give up their weekends and holiday vacations to attend practices. And many student managers, including Duke's, do all this hard work without getting paid or receive a very small stipend.

Still there are some serious benefits for those lucky enough to land a student manager gig. Many managers past and present have pursued a career in sports. They have become coaches, equipment managers, directors of scouting, and directors of operations. After he graduates from Duke, Kelly plans to pursue a career in sports physical therapy.

LEARN ABOUT THE
BUSINESS OF SPORTS

If a student plans to pursue a sports personnel career, he or she can start learning about the business side of sports while still in high school. Students can stay up-to-date on the latest industry news by reading sports journals and blogs, and by following key industry social media accounts. Many media outlets present articles, television segments, social media features, or interviews that present information about different business topics in sports. For example, Forbes.com has a section of its website called SportsMoney, which is dedicated to covering news on the business of sports. On sites like Sports-Money, students can read a variety of business-focused articles, such as information about the MLB's new ad campaigns or the valuations of world soccer teams.

Abraham Madkour, the executive editor of the *SportsBusiness Journal/Daily* predicts that coverage of sports business will only grow in the future. "There will be more and more coverage of the sports business from all forms of media. You will see more coverage from the mainstream media and non-traditional media. The reason is because sports business, as an industry, continues on a major growth trajectory and there is a massive amount of interest around it," he said in an article on the Fields of Green website.

VOLUNTEER FOR TEAMS AND EVENTS

Volunteering is another great way to gain experience in the sports industry. Students can volunteer with community teams, coaching younger players. They can also volunteer to help with planning special events, such as organizing a baseball or hockey tournament or helping out at a fund-raiser to benefit a local team. Working as a volunteer, a high school student gains valuable experience and makes contacts with adults who may be able to provide a reference or recommendation when he or she applies for a job or internship in the future.

While in college, Morgan Ranier decided to pursue volunteer opportunities in golf for the summer, a sport she knew little about. Because she had no contacts in the golf industry, she used the internet to contact a few Professional Golfers' Association (PGA) events. "I kept the e-mails brief but communicated that I was a student who was hungry for experience in the sports industry and that I was a hard worker who is willing to roll up my sleeves and get things done. I would then attach my résumé that outlined my experiences and skill set," said Ranier in an interview posted on the Kristi Dosh website. Ranier received many responses to her emails and invitations to help at different PGA events. She volunteered at several events, with two becoming paid event contract positions. One of her volunteer PGA events was the HP Byron Nelson Championship in Irving, Texas. Some of the other volunteers were long-time members of the AT&T Cotton Bowl staff. Ranier jumped right into the work and had fun working with the other volunteers, the PGA staff, and members of the media. By the end of the week, Ranier was invited to be part of the volunteer team for the AT&T Cotton Bowl. A few years later, Ranier turned her volunteer experience into a full-time job. She landed a job as the assistant director of marketing and communications at the AT&T Cotton Bowl Classic.

Country music superstar Carrie Underwood winds up to throw a pitch at a celebrity softball game, an event organized by many volunteers and professionals.

WORK AS AN OFFICIAL

Working as an official, referee, or umpire can boost any student's résumé. Working as an official in some capacity shows leadership. Whether it is a volunteer position or a paid job, the experience is valuable. Learning the nuances of officiating can help a student understand new aspects of a familiar sport. As an official gains experience, he or she may advance to higher levels and may supervise less experienced officials.

Matt Killiany is the umpire coordinator for the Kirkwood Athletic Association in Missouri. He believes that teens

A young man volunteers as a referee and hands out shirts and explains the rules to participants before an intramural indoor soccer game.

should consider becoming umpires or other types of sport officials because they receive many benefits from the experience. "Character building, I think, is one of the biggest benefits," said Killiany in an article posted on Engage Sports .com. "As an umpire, you have to be in charge and keep a clear head in pressure situations. That's a skill that can be a huge benefit in life beyond the baseball diamond."

Working as an official can also help teens build contacts in the sports world. Young officials typically work with coordinators and get to know league coaches and their staff. They attend training and courses with other people with similar interests and career goals. Building a list of professional contacts, even at an early age, can pay off in future years.

SUMMER LEARNING

Some colleges offer summer programs for high school students to prepare for future careers in sports. For example, Drexel University in Philadelphia offers a one-week program for motivated high school students to learn about career possibilities in several fields, including sports management. Also in Philadelphia, the Wharton Sports Business Academy (WSBA) is a four-week summer program that

At the University of Pennsylvania's Wharton School of Business, high school students can study sports business leadership during a summer program.

gives talented high school juniors and seniors the opportunity to study sports business leadership at the University of Pennsylvania's Wharton School. In the program, students learn about ownership, marketing, media, and labor while they meet and learn from leaders in the sports business world. Many other colleges, including Saint Louis University, Syracuse University, UCLA, and Georgetown University offer sport business summer programs.

Currently a sports management major at the University of Michigan, Emmy Latham attended the Wharton Sports Business Academy in 2014. An avid sports fan, she decided to give the summer program a try. At WSBA, Latham worked on an original business plan and presentation. "My time at WSBA was the key to my decision to pursue Sport Management. I deeply enjoyed the relationships I built, topics we studied, and visits we made to leading companies in the sport industry," she said in an interview posted on the Julian Krinsky Camps & Programs website. Latham credits the WSBA for leading her to pursue a career in sports. Now at the University of Michigan, she has joined the Michigan Sport Business Association and other sport business organizations. She has also worked in an internship with the Michigan Athletic Department and is a writer and content producer for the 2017 Michigan Sport Business Conference. "This involvement all stems from my experience at WSBA, where guest lectures and company visits providing insight into the industry inspired me to take full advantage of opportunities for experience in and outside of the classroom," she said in the Julian Krinsky interview. After graduation, Latham hopes to work one day for the National Hockey League in hockey operations, community relations, or a related position.

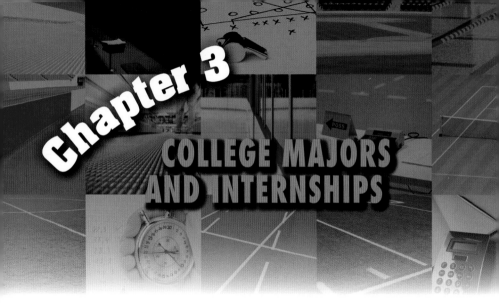

Chapter 3

COLLEGE MAJORS AND INTERNSHIPS

For students interested in sports personnel careers, there are many options. Some people major in business, hospitality and recreation, communications, or management. Those pursuing specialized careers such as accounting or law generally major in finance, accounting, or prelaw studies.

However, for the majority of students considering a career in sports personnel, a degree in sports management is a great start. Depending on the areas of interest and intended career path, students can specialize in different aspects of sports personnel, from accounting and finance to marketing and media relations.

SPORTS MANAGEMENT DEGREE

Earning a sports management degree is a great way to prepare a student for a career in sports personnel. The study and classes required for a sports management degree provide students with the basic knowledge and skills in finance, management, marketing, and the law as it relates to organization in the sports industry. The program prepares students to work with different levels of sports organization, including amateur, collegiate, and professional sports organizations. Sometimes, a sports management degree can be offered as a combined degree program with business, finance, law, health, or other field.

Across the United States, there are approximately three hundred undergraduate sports management programs, one hundred and fifty master's degree programs, and twenty-five to thirty doctoral programs, according to the North American Society for Sports Management. These programs include sports business programs such as facility management, sport marketing, sport law, intercollegiate athletics, and professional and minor league sports. These programs prepare students to use critical thinking and strategies to solve real-world problems in the sports industry. "The benefit of a sport management degree is that it provides the student with a basic foundation of the sport business," says John Wolohan, a professor and graduate program director of the Sport Venue and Event Management program at Syracuse University, in an article on WorkInSports.com. "It takes the student from being a fan, and teaches them that there is more to the sports business than rooting for your team."

In a sports management program, students will generally take core classes in management, economics,

Marketing professionals collaborate and gather information from drivers and crew to design a new publicity promotion for a Formula One racing team.

financial accounting, algebra, general psychology, and physical or biological science. They may also take courses in statistics and public speaking. Students will also take sports management courses that focus on various aspects of the industry, such as business finance, sport facility design and management, sports marketing, ethics and sports, and legal issues in sports.

TWO-YEAR AND FOUR-YEAR DEGREES

There are several types of degrees available for students studying sports management. Associate's degree programs are broad based and focus on the fundamentals of fields such as physical education, coaching, management and business ethics, and law. Some associate's degrees focus on accounting or finance. These programs typically take two years to complete.

Most students choose to pursue a bachelor's degree at a four-year college or university. Students pursuing a bachelor's degree in sports management may choose to specialize in certain areas within the field, such as marketing, business administration, accounting, risk management, or fitness and wellness.

Amanda Dinkel graduated in 2013 from North Carolina State University with a degree in sports management. Today, she works as a community relations

Atlanta Falcons quarterback Matt Ryan prepares to receive the ball during Super Bowl LI on February 5, 2017, against the New England Patriots.

manager with the National Football League's Atlanta Falcons. In 2017, she went to the Super Bowl with the Falcons. She firmly believes that earning her degree in sports management prepared her for her current career with the Atlanta Falcons. "The variety of courses I took at NC State were very helpful in preparing me for this career, especially with all the projects we had to do. I know we all moaned and groaned when we had to do a project in class, but those projects ended up helping me more than I ever thought they would. I kept all my projects I worked on while in sport management and showcased them during my interview process to show my interviewers the skills I had learned. I also had amazing professors that did a great job preparing me, and I had so many great opportunities while I was in school that helped me build a solid résumé. My professors and advisors were always supportive and helpful during my time in school, especially with career advice. I also learned while getting my degree that experience is key. I did multiple internships during my time at NC State, which was just the right start to my career," she said in an article posted on the North Carolina State University website.

ADVANCED DEGREES

Some students choose to pursue advanced degrees in sports management. Master's degree programs prepare students for higher level management and administrative roles. Generally, students earn either a master's in business administration (MBA) or a master's of science. An MBA degree with a concentration in finance, marketing, or sports management prepares students for leadership roles in the industry. "The MBA in Sport Management combines sport-specific classes with the breadth and depth of MBA classes. This unique combination gives you the ability to master the various aspects of the sport business," said Mark Hecox, chair of the sports management department at Southern New Hampshire University, in an article posted on the Southern New Hampshire University website.

A master's of science in sports management prepares students for a career in sports management at all levels, from recreational sports to professional leagues. Graduates are often hired to work in roles such as sports administrator, corporate sponsorship director, head coach, or general manager. Beyond master's programs, a few students choose to earn a doctorate degree in sports management.

Greg Gosselin chose to earn his master's of science in sport management in an online program at Southern New Hampshire University. "When I first graduated with my undergraduate degree in general business, I wasn't really satisfied so I went back and got my degree in sport management," he said in an article on the Southern New Hampshire University website. "I came to SNHU to change my career and now I work for a professional hockey team... to be happy to get up every morning and go to a job that I love to do is something that I would never exchange."

JOB SHADOWING

Job shadowing is another way to learn more about a sports career. Students learn about a job by walking through a workday with a sports professional. Students see firsthand a person doing his or her job, learning about the work environment and the skills required. A job shadowing experience can be as simple as an hour visit with a single person. Alternatively, it can be a week-long experience with interaction with several staff members and observation of a variety of tasks.

Brittany Holen, a senior studying sports business at Grand Canyon University in Phoenix, Arizona, job shadowed Nebraska employees one day during a Nebraska Huskers football game against Iowa. Holen helped the stadium staff salt sidewalks, set up gates and tables, check the radio, assist security, and help to keep fans happy and engaged. Even though it

A young professional in the sports industry explains a memo she has prepared to a woman who is job shadowing her for the day.

was only eleven degrees and freezing rain, the experience gave her a firsthand look into the work it takes to get a venue ready for a college football game.

There are many career options for students who earn a sports management degree. Some of the most popular jobs for students with sports management degrees are in sales, analytics, public relations, management, business development, social media, and consulting. They work to become athletic trainers, college athletic administrators, operations managers, team marketers, team managers, sales specialists, directors of communications, or sports event planners. Some students choose careers with a focus in fitness and nutrition. Regardless, a sports management degree provides a great foundation for a career in sports.

INTERNSHIPS

In addition to a degree, many students get real-life experience in the sports industry by working in an internship. Interns can work in a variety of roles and departments, including athletic administration, sports marketing and promotion, media publicity and relations, sports law, event planning, or sports medicine and athletic training.

Working as an intern gives students the opportunity to gain experience and learn about different specialties and sports personnel careers, whether it is working in the marketing department or helping plan sporting events. This experience is so valuable, some sports management programs even include it as one of the graduation requirements. In addition to gaining experience, interns also make valuable contacts with other sports professionals that may be useful in future job searches.

Landing an internship, getting experience, and working hard are essential steps for a career in sports personnel. Carolyne Savini is the senior vice president of recruiting at Turnkey Sports and Entertainment, a sports recruiting firm. She emphasizes internships are a necessity for anyone interested in working in the sports industry. "For anyone trying to break into the sports industry at the entry level, internship experience is critical. Short of an inside connection, I rarely, if ever, see someone get hired into a job without previous in-

A Clemson Tigers player wears Nike basketball shoes during a college basketball game against the Syracuse Orange in 2016 at the Carrier Dome in Syracuse, New York.

ternship experience. The reason is the sports industry is a small, tight-knit community. One can't hide from a reference. If an employer sees the résumé of someone who worked for a team or agency property down the street, a call will be made prior to an interview ever being scheduled to confirm how hard and smart of a worker the applicant is," she said in an article posted on Forbes.com.

A former high school basketball player, Taylor Winston is studying sports business at Grand Canyon University in Phoenix, Arizona. She worked in a summer internship for the Nike Chi-League tournament in Chicago, assisting the head event coordinator. "I got to sit in meetings with the Nike Chicago brand manager, products marketing manager, and basketball event coordinator," she said in an article posted on WorkInSports.com. "I was only 19, but I was sitting with these huge people, and they would ask my opinion. I realized I wanted to do sports event planning. It was a cool moment." After she returned to Arizona after the end of the summer internship, Winston got a call from the tournament marketing manager asking if she could return for another week. Nike paid for her hotel and flight for her to come back. On her return, she managed the kids' court, scheduling, planning, and marketing. And as a bonus, she got to meet NBA players Joakim Noah, Scottie Pippen, and Anthony Davis.

Students can find sports internships in a variety of place. Most agencies, organizations, and institutions at all levels of sport hire a number of interns each semester and

A manager explains a project to a young intern who is participating in a summer internship program to gain experience in the sports industry.

over the summer to help run their operations. Professional sports organizations often offer intern programs. For example, the National Basketball Association internship program is a ten-week summer program where interns learn about the NBA, WNBA, and NBA D-League. In the National Hockey League, each team runs its own internship program. For example, the New York Rangers and the Madison Square Garden Company Associate Program hire undergraduate and graduate student interns to work in all areas of the business, including MSG Sports, MSG Media, MSG Entertainment, and corporate divisions.

Chapter 4

PUBLIC, MEDIA, AND COMMUNITY RELATIONS

In November 2016, the Detroit Pistons and Palace Sports and Entertainment joined forces with Forgotten Harvest, a Detroit food bank, to transform the Piston's arena, the Palace of Auburn Hills, into a festive dining room and a Thanksgiving feast for more than seven hundred community guests. The entire Detroit Pistons team, coaching staff, and thirty active servicemen and servicewomen helped out and served meals to guests. After dinner, there was music, an appearance from the Piston's mascot Hooper, and a kids' zone with basketball hoops, cookie decorating, and a photo booth. "The dinner is very special to all of the families but the experience and presence of the Detroit Pistons is by far the most exciting part of the evening for everyone," said Kirk Mayes, CEO of Forgotten Harvest in an article on the Forgotten Harvest website. "This opportunity for these kids to see players that they idolize in person is a memory they will never forget."

The Detroit Pistons celebrate after winning at the Palace of Auburn Hills. The arena is also used to host several team community relations events.

Events like these are organized by Heather Collart, the director of community relations for the Detroit Pistons. On event days, she and her team go through high level run-throughs of each aspect of the event, troubleshoot any problems that arise, and get everything set up and ready to go. She says that many people assist to make events successful, with everything from public relations coverage to having the right audio/visual equipment on hand. The annual Thanksgiving event is a special one for Collart. "Seeing how excited everyone was and thankful to have a special meal meant a lot to personally have planned and executed that event. Just as important was seeing how much fun our athletes, their families and our staff had serving these people—which only further demonstrates how fun and inspiring volunteer work can be," she said in an article on WorkInSports.com.

For students interested in public, media, or community relations, there are many opportunities in sports, in areas such as public and media relations, event marketing, community relations, and working for sports public relations and athletic firms. A public relations (PR) representative ensures that a client, such as a team, league, athlete, or company, has a good and strong reputation with the general public. PR representatives search the internet for any references to their client. They follow breaking news in the media and look for any potential problems or issues for their client. PR specialists also work with a variety of media outlets, from newspapers to television, to release important stories about their clients. Every time a client signs a new contract, works with a new sponsor, or releases a branded product, the PR specialist writes a press release to let the public know about it.

Other PR people prefer to work in event marketing. They typically work for sports complexes, basketball arenas, baseball fields, and other sports facilities. They come up with advertising and marketing for upcoming events at these venues. They also design and market special promotional events to draw in fans, such as fireworks nights, free T-shirt days, and other events.

A community relations manager coordinates an organization's charity and community fund-raising efforts. These people organize player appearances, manage donation requests, participate in auctions, and coordinate special events. Community relations managers also write and edit news releases and work with local journalists to get coverage about the team's good works into media outlets.

Some people who work in public relations work directly for companies that manufacture sports equipment, shoes and clothing, and anything else athletes need. They write press releases to tell people about new products or changes in existing products. They design campaigns to entice shoppers to buy the company's products. They may also work on advertising campaigns before a new product is available in stores to build interest. These campaigns can include television, radio, print, and internet ads.

JOB TASKS

People working in public, media, and community relations create and maintain a favorable public image for the organization, team, company, or athlete they represent. They create media releases to promote a positive public image of their client and to increase public awareness about achievements, work in the community, and goals.

A soccer team manager and player attend a press conference before a European soccer match, an event organized by the team's media relations department.

On the job, these specialists often perform the following tasks:

- Write press releases and prepare information for the media

- Prepare a response to an information request from the media

- Search through the internet, social media sites, and other media sources for news about their organization and information about the organization's public image

- Write speeches for top executives

- Arrange for media interviews with top executives and athletes

- Create and evaluate advertising and promotion campaigns to determine if they match the organization's public relations goals

- Use social media to publicize and promote an organization

- Organize events for charities and fund-raising

Also known as media specialists, public relations specialists are responsible for all of an organization's communications with the public, such as customers, fans, investors, reporters, and other PR specialists. They draft press releases and talk to reporters and others in the media who might print or broadcast their information. Often, a newspaper or magazine article or television special report begins in the hands of a public relations specialist.

As more people use the internet and social media, public relations specialists are often responsible for monitoring websites, social media sites, chat rooms, and more for posts and questions about their organization. They can quickly interact with fans and customers by answering questions or addressing concerns on social media sites.

EDUCATIONAL AND PROFESSIONAL REQUIREMENTS

Most public relations specialists have a bachelor's degree from a four-year college or university. Many employers prefer candidates with a degree in sports management, public relations, journalism, communications, English, or business. Through these programs, students can build a portfolio of work and writing that they can use to demonstrate their abilities to potential employers.

Having some related experience can make a candidate stand out to employers. Some students work in

Pitcher Ariel Miranda of the Seattle Mariners meets with catcher Carlos Ruiz and the team's infield players at the pitcher's mound during a game against the Houston Astros.

internships at public relations firms or in the public relations departments of sports organizations. Others gain experience in communications by working on a school newspaper or holding a leadership position in school or in the community. All of these experiences allow students to develop skills that will be helpful in landing a job as a public relations specialist for a sports organization.

While in college at the University of Washington, Krista Staudinger landed an internship in the communications and public relations department of the Seattle Mariners, a Major League Baseball team. As an intern, Staudinger pulled sports clips from local newspapers. She provided information about Seattle to the visiting team's public relations department and traveling media. She edited materials from press releases, game notes, and the Mariners monthly magazine. She also wrote original articles for the magazine and Mariners public relations blog. In addition, Staudinger created scorecards, assisted with press conferences, and helped to prepare the press box. She says that confidence, communication, and organization are essential skills for students considering careers in sports public relations. "You have to be confident in yourself and your skills and not intimidated to speak with the media and athletes. Strong communication skills are also very important, especially for handling media requests. As most job descriptions require, being highly organized and being able to work on multiple tasks at a time will go a long way!" she said in an article posted on WorkInSports.

SOCIAL MEDIA MANAGER

The rise of social media has opened doors for a new type of job—a social media manager. Companies in all industries, including sports, are finding that social media specialists are needed to manage their online reputations. Social media managers monitor a team's social media accounts across several platforms, such as Facebook, Instagram, and Twitter. On these platforms, they communicate with the public.

Using technical skills, social media managers create and post memorable content, such as images, text, or videos, in order to spark interest in the team or organization. They create memorable GIFs, manipulate images using Photoshop, and edit videos so that they can be posted on all social media platforms. They might share photos from a team event or the latest game. Sometimes they work with the marketing department to publicize an upcoming event. Fans can like, comment, repost, and retweet their favorite content.

Social media managers measure the effectiveness of their posts by tracking how many times a post is shared. They can also use online tools to analyze the results on social media platforms and fan engagement.

com. After her internship and graduation, Staudinger landed a full-time job in the Australian Baseball League. She says her internship was an invaluable experience. "My internship with the Mariners helped prepare me for my role with the Australian Baseball League because I was able to see firsthand how a major league club runs its media relations and social media platforms," she said in the WorkInSports.com article. "I was essentially in charge of facilitating the media relations and social media accounts for the league in Australia, so it was helpful to know best practices from the Mariners and have experience in the field."

Once hired, public relations specialists often learn important skills on the job. Entry-level workers typically are responsible for maintaining files, searching media articles and sources, and gathering information for speeches and pamphlets. After they have mastered these experiences, they may be assigned additional responsibilities, such as writing news releases, speeches, and articles, or handling public relations programs.

WORK ENVIRONMENT

Public relations specialists typically work in an office environment. They do have some travel to deliver speeches and to attend meetings and community events. Most work full time during regular business hours. Before a big event or product launch or when dealing with an unexpected public image problem, these employees often work long hours to get the job done, including evenings and weekends.

OPPORTUNITIES FOR ADVANCEMENT

Experienced public relations specialists usually get to take on more responsibility and work on complex projects. Senior specialists may supervise teams of employees on

A public relations manager goes through an airport security check on his way to a meeting with colleagues across the country.

a large project. Some specialists may advance to higher level positions, such as director of public relations. Others might leave an organization and start their own consulting company.

Experienced public relations specialists with a track record of excellent work are more likely to be considered for a promotion. In addition, those who have a master's degree in business administration, communications, sports management, or a related field are also likely to have more opportunities to advance.

JOB OUTLOOK

According to the Bureau of Labor Services (BLS), the employment of public relations specialists across all industries is expected to grow 6 percent over the next several years. This rate is approximately as fast as the average rate for all occupations. This growth will be driven by the need of organizations to promote community outreach and customer relations in order to improve their visibility in the community and maintain and enhance their reputation with the public. Because of the speed of the internet and social media, good and bad news about an organization can spread around the world at lightning speed. As a result, public relations specialists will be needed to respond to news as it happens and manage their organization's public image.

The growing popularity of social media is expected to increase the need for public relations specialists in all industries, including sports. Social media is an entirely new branch of media that creates new tasks and responsibilities for an organization's public relations department. Specialists who are experienced using social media platforms will be in demand to appeal to fans, consumers, and the general public using these digital mediums. Public relations specialists will be

A public relations manager checks his cell phone and his team's social media feeds as he works on his laptop at a local coffee shop.

needed to develop a plan for organizations to use social media efficiently and effectively.

Because jobs in public relations are highly desirable, the competition for open positions can be strong. Students with experience in public relations and communications and a strong portfolio of past work will have the best opportunities.

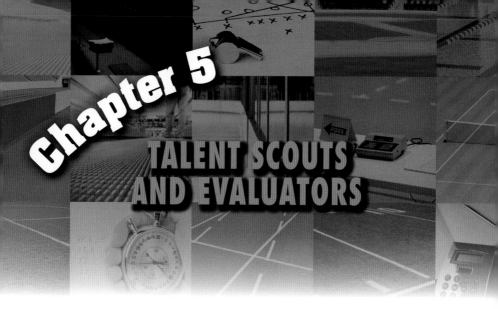

Chapter 5

TALENT SCOUTS AND EVALUATORS

In the days and weeks leading up to the NFL Draft, the real work of an NFL scout begins. Every winter, scouts from each NFL team converge on the NFL Scouting Combine, a week-long showcase where college players hoping to be drafted by an NFL team perform physical and mental tests. Like many other teams, the Seattle Seahawks have a large group of scouts, coaches, and talent evaluators at the combine, including Scott Fitterer and Trent Kirchner, codirectors of player personnel. Each day of the 2017 combine they arrive at Lucas Oil Stadium, ready for a long day of evaluating players.

As the players warm up on the field, Fitterer, senior personnel executive Ed Dodds, and director of college scouting Matt Berry head down to the field. They sit in the stands at the 40-yard-line with stopwatches in hand. As each player runs, they clock his time with their handheld watches and call up the times to another scout who records them on a computer. The Seahawks will use these stopwatch times to

Head coach Rex Ryan of the New York Jets celebrates in the locker room after the football team's win against the Miami Dolphins.

compare against times recorded at players' pro days with the team. While the work can be a little monotonous, the men do what they can to have fun. When a player false starts, the three hold up their stopwatches to see who was the quickest to start and stop the clock. The scouts also pick who will run the fastest in each position group. This morning Berry celebrates when his pick, TCU's Aviante Collins, runs the fastest time for offensive linemen.

From one of the stadium's suites, Kirchner and several of Seattle's scouts and coaches watch players run the 40-yard dash and go through position workouts. When a player posts a workout number that is an outlier, Kirchner pulls up a spreadsheet in seconds to show Seattle head coach Pete Carroll how players who posted similar results ultimately performed in the NFL.

On the field, other scouts help organize drills. National scout Josh Graff measures players in the broad jump, while Aaron Hineline, an area scout, leads a group of players around the field, making sure they get to where they need to be. He keeps the day moving efficiently and also gets a chance to learn a little more about each player as he spends time with them.

After the on-the-field workouts are finished for the day, the group heads back to their hotel prepared for a long night of work. In the early evening, players rotate through hotel rooms, interviewing with different NFL teams. Before Seattle's first interview, the room fills with scouts and coaches. Fitterer and Kirchner stay in the room the entire time for all the player interviews. In the short time allotted for each player, scouts and coaches fire questions, asking about everything from a player's childhood to his knowledge of offensive or defensive systems. Throughout it all, Fitterer and Kirchner scribble notes and whisper their observations. When a player's time is up, an air horn goes off in the lobby. A new player enters the room and the process begins all over again. More than twelve hours after they started the day, the Seahawks scouts have finished five interviews, but they are not even halfway done for the night. As Kirchner says in a March 2017 article on Seahawks.com, "The fun is just getting started."

For Kirchner, Fitterer, and the rest of the Seattle scouts, evaluations will continue at the combine and at pro days at various college campuses. By the time the April NFL draft arrives in April, the Seattle scouts and coaches will be ready to select the team's next group of players.

JOB TASKS

A sports or athletic scout is a person who helps college and professional teams find the best athletes in the world. Scouts work for all of the major sporting league—NFL, MLB, NBA, NHL, as well as international soccer leagues. They work for scouting companies and colleges to identify and recruit top high school athletes. And some scouts have even started representing high school players to colleges, helping them land a valuable scholarship to school.

Scouts travel around the state, country, and world to watch athletes perform. They evaluate the athletic ability and potential of amateur and professional players. They also monitor news sources for information about athletes, attend games, and talk to coaches about promising athletes. Scouts study game films and statistics to learn more about athletes and determine their potential. Scouts can be self-employed or work for a college, professional team, or scouting organization. A scout's job typically involves:

A talent scout scans the local newspaper to gather information about athletes that he will be observing later that day and enters notes into his laptop.

- Reading newspapers and other news sources to find athletes to consider

- Attending games, viewing videotapes of the athletes' performances, and studying statistics about the athletes to determine talent and potential

- Talking to athletes and coaches to see if the athlete has what it takes to succeed

71

THE RISE OF DATA ANALYTICS IN SCOUTING

In the past, sports teams made decisions about which players to recruit, retain, and trade based on scouting reports and visual assessments of a player's abilities. In recent years, the use of data analytics to drive these decisions is growing in popularity. Data analytics examines large amounts of data and statistics about players to determine patterns and make predictions about future performance. Most major professional sports teams have data analytics experts, sometimes even an entire department. Teams can scan scout notes into computer files, which data developers and mathematicians use to crunch the numbers and create player profiles. This information can be used to determine if a team should draft a player, sign a free agent, or trade for one. However, data analytics are not foolproof. Data cannot measure a player's heart, drive, or mental toughness. Recognizing this, most teams that use data analytics do not rely on them exclusively. Instead, information from data analytics becomes one piece of information in the team's player evaluations.

- Reporting to the coach, manager, or owner of the team for which he or she is scouting

- Arranging for and offering incentives to prospective players

EDUCATIONAL AND PROFESSIONAL REQUIREMENTS

People who become sports scouts are usually very passionate about a sport. Many scouts also have a business background, as organizations want scouts who are able to analyze stacks of statistics and turn it into meaningful information and analysis for teams.

A baseball scout records statistics about prospective players. Later these statistics will be entered into a computer program for data analysis.

Many organizations, such as colleges and professional teams, require scouts to have a bachelor's degree, although some organizations require a candidate to have only a high school diploma. Students who earn a bachelor's degree often major in business, marketing, sales, or sports management. To prepare for a career as a sports scout, students can take classes in mathematics, statistics, and business. For those who choose to pursue an associate's or bachelor's degree, programs in business, sports management, marketing, and other sports-related fields are preferred. In these programs, they will typically take classes in finance, marketing, business law, accounting, management, contract negotiation, and the sociology of sports. Some people choose to earn a master's or doctorate in sports management.

Often, an in-depth knowledge of a sport is as important for scouts as a formal education. Scouting jobs typically do not require a candidate to have experience playing a sport in college or in a professional league, but it can help. They must have a good eye to identify talent, a skill that usually comes from playing or coaching the sport for several years. Scouts should have an eye for detail and strong interpersonal skills to develop relationships with players, coaches, and other scouts.

Joey Clinkscales is the director of player personnel for the National Football League's Oakland Raiders. He had a short career as an NFL wide receiver in the late 1980s before becoming a pro scout. He says that he looks for specific skills when hiring new scouts for his organization. "Anybody can grade the good guys," Clinkscales said in an article on NFL Player Engagement.com. "It's the other guys. Maybe this guy isn't ready, but he has the skill set. You have to understand why something happened. We look for guys that understand concepts and can explain why something's happening. Those guys that can articulate that on paper would be the ones I would hire first."

WORK ENVIRONMENT

Scouts can work for a variety of organizations. Some scouts work for scouting organizations that deal with high school athletes, collecting information on the athlete and helping promote him or her to colleges and universities. Other scouts work for scouting organizations that help colleges find and recruit top high school athletes. At the professional level, scouts generally work directly for a team or organization. According to the BLS, approximately 10 percent of scouts were self-employed in 2014.

Because many events take place outdoors, scouts are expected to work in all weather conditions. During the busy season, scouts work long hours, including evenings, weekends, and holidays. Although the idea of travel appeals to some people, scouts often make sacrifices in their personal life and are frequently away from home because of the job's travel schedule.

OPPORTUNITIES FOR ADVANCEMENT

Many people start in this career as a part-time or volunteer scout. Once they have gained experience as an unpaid intern, they can advance to paying jobs as regional scouts or assistants to regional scouts. Over time, they can advance to become a head scout for a region or a team, managing other scouts.

Curt Miller, the head coach of the WNBA's Connecticut Sun, sits on the bench with assistant coach Nicki Collen during a game against the San Antonio Stars.

Sometimes, knowing the right person can lead to a scouting job. Networking within the scouting world is a great way to prepare for this career and can lead to future job opportunities. Students who spend a summer working with a local coach or scout, even to run errands, can make valuable contacts for the future.

Thomas Dimitroff, the general manager of the Atlanta Falcons, began his career as a scout for the Saskatchewan Roughriders of the Canadian Football League (CFL). After college, Dimitroff wanted to be a football coach, like his father. But he decided to give scouting a try when Dan Rambo, the Roughriders' assistant general manager who Dimitroff had known for years, offered him a job in 1990. "I was a scout, but I was a lackey. I did everything they needed me to do from a personnel standpoint. Teams in the CFL, you know, are so much more scaled down from what they're doing here in the NFL, so I was doing so many different things. I had a really close relationship with the coaches, so I sort of satisfied my needs and wants. But still, I was way down the totem pole...But I made great friends there. It was a great opportunity," he said in an article for the *Toronto Sun*. As he gained experience, Dimitroff found that he enjoyed scouting more and more. As part of his job, he attended several NFL training camps, looking for players who might be cut and would want to play in the CFL. "My dad was in the NFL at that point, but I was meeting more and more people now, not only through him, but on my own. Getting my foot in the door. So when I was travelling around, I got the chance to talk a lot of football with all of these good NFL people. That was invaluable," he said in the article for the *Toronto Sun*.

After a brief stint with the World League of American Football and a corporate league football team in Japan, Dimitroff returned to the United States and ended up working for the Cleveland Browns' ground crew, while also writing scouting reports part-time for the Kansas City Chiefs. While working at the Browns, Dimitroff met Scott Pioli, a rising scout. "Here I'd have paint all over me, smelling like I'd been traveling Europe for 10 days, and

Scott and I would just talk football," Dimitroff said in an article for the *Los Angeles Times.* "That was the beginning of a really cool and deep relationship with Scott."

After a few months, Dimitroff landed a full-time scouting position with the Detroit Lions. A few years later, he advanced to a college scouting position with the Cleveland Browns and by 2002 was hired as a national scout by the New England Patriots. A year later, in 2003, Dimitroff was promoted to the director of college scouting for the Patriots, working for his friend Scott Pioli, who was the Patriots' vice president of player personnel at the time. And then in 2007, he was named the general manager of the Atlanta Falcons.

JOB OUTLOOK

Growing interest in college and professional sports is expected to increase the demand for scouts. According to the Bureau of Labor Statistics, jobs for athletic coaches and scouts are expected to grow six percent over the next decade. This rate is about the same as the average for all occupations. Because competitive athletic programs help colleges recruit future students and athletes and encourage alumni donations, colleges are increasingly turning to scouts to find the most talented high school athletes. As participation in high school and college sports increases, the demand for coaches and scouts is also expected to increase. Many small, Division III colleg-

An NFL scout from the San Francisco 49ers records notes after watching players perform drills during pro day at the University of Colorado Boulder.

es are adding new athletic teams to promote schools and recruit students. In addition, the growth in women's sports creates a need for more college scouts. As college tuition rises and athletic scholarships become more competitive, more high school athletes are expected to hire scouts directly to increase their likelihood of receiving a college scholarship. Job prospects for this career should be good, although strong competition is expected for higher-paying jobs with colleges and professional teams.

Chapter 6

BUSINESS OFFICE CAREERS

B ehind the scenes, people in the sports business office take care of the day-to-day tasks of running a sports organization. Like any other industry, sports organizations need accountants to track revenues and expenses; human resources specialists to handle hiring, benefits, and other employee concerns; and a legal team to review contracts, leases, and season ticket agreements.

LEGAL COUNSEL

The business of sports is growing every year, and with it, the legal issues facing organizations. These include media rights deals, streaming rights, player contracts, managing arenas and stadium, negotiating with corporate sponsors, contracts for luxury suite leases, and seat-license sales. "The business is just growing in scale," said Glenn Wong, professor in the Isenberg School of Management at the University of Massachusetts and president of the Sports Lawyers Association, in an article for the *Sports Business Journal*. "When there's more at stake, there are more legal issues. People take it more seriously."

As deals have become more complex, teams are hiring more in-house legal experts. Many sports franchises have at least two full-time lawyers and several interns to handle daily legal tasks. Often it's not enough to keep up. The New York Yankees have eight in-house attorneys. Lonn Trost,

Baseball player Alex Rodriguez from the New York Yankees arrives with his legal counsel at Major League Baseball's offices in Manhattan.

the Yankees chief operating officer and general counsel, says they still can't keep up with the flood of contracts and legal matters that come through the office on a daily basis.

Sports lawyers deal with everything from employment law to risk management. "The diversity of issues is tremendous," said Nona Lee, Arizona Diamondbacks general counsel in an article for the *Sports Business Journal*. "That's one of the things I love about it."

A LAWYER IN THE NHL

Contracts, sponsorship agreements, and arena renovations are just some of the legal work that Danna Haydar, associate general counsel for the NHL's Tampa Bay Lightning, Amalie Arena, and a sister Arena Football League franchise, handles. Although the local government owns the building, the team runs the arena. "As a girl who grew up in Toronto, I'm a huge hockey fan," Haydar said in an article for the Sports Business Journal. *"And I always wanted to be in law. The icing on the cake is living in a place with palm trees." On a typical day, Haydar juggles several projects, such as an agreement related to a newly installed statue in front of the arena, contract items for an upcoming Garth Brooks concert, a few sponsorship deals, waivers for a dog night at an arena football game, and monitoring contracts for a $25 million arena renovation.*

She shares lengthy to-do list with the Lightning's general counsel, Jim Shimberg. Whatever the two lawyers cannot handle is outsourced to an outside law firm.

LEGAL COUNSEL: EDUCATIONAL AND PROFESSIONAL REQUIREMENTS

Becoming a sports lawyer requires several years of college and law school. Students must first earn a bachelor's degree from a four-year college or university. Prelaw students often take classes in English, public speaking, government, history, economics, and mathematics. Those interested in sports law should also take sports management coursework.

After earning a bachelor's degree, students must then move on to three years of law school where they will earn a juris doctor (JD) degree from a law school accredited by the American Bar Association (ABA). Almost all law schools require prospective students to take the Law School Admission Test (LSAT), a standardized test that measures a student's aptitude for studying law. In law school, students will take courses in constitutional law, contracts, property law, civil procedure, and legal writing. They may also choose to specialize in areas such as taxes, labor, and corporate law.

Once students graduate from law school, they must then take a licensing exam called a bar exam in the state in which they intend to practice law. If they pass the test, they receive their license to practice law. The requirements to practice law vary by state and jurisdictions. Most states require lawyers to graduate from an accredited law school, pass a written bar exam, and be found by the state's admitting board to be of good character. Lawyers who plan to practice law in more than one state may have to take the bar exam in multiple states. In addition, most states required lawyers to take continuing education classes to stay current with recent developments in the law.

JOB OUTLOOK FOR LEGAL COUNSEL

According to the BLS's *Occupational Outlook Handbook*, lawyer jobs are projected to increase over the next several years. Demand for legal work is expected to continue as organizations of all types, including those in the sports industry, need legal services. While many companies will hire law firms to handle legal work, an increasing number of organizations will hire more in-house legal counsel to lower costs. For many organizations, it is more economical to hire full-time legal staff than to outsource work to outside lawyers.

Competition for legal jobs with sports organizations is expected to be strong as more students graduate from law school. Candidates with a strong legal background and related experience in the sports industry will have the best chances of landing a position with a sports organization.

HUMAN RESOURCES SPECIALIST

Every company needs a human resources (HR) department to manage its employees, especially a sports organization. Sports is a people business, and human resources specialists focus on the people in an organization. HR specialists work for both league offices and individual teams. HR specialists recruit people to come work for the organization. Although the coaching staff generally selects the players on the field, there are many other people needed to make a sports organization successful. Sports teams often have to deal with seasonal hiring for stadium or arena staff, along with personnel for ticketing offices, security, stadium operations, and guest services. These positions may require drug testing, background checks, credit checks, and criminal history checks, all of which HR is responsible for obtaining. HR professionals may also handle compensation and benefits, training and development, and employee assistance programs that help employees deal with problems that affect their work.

HR specialists often screen potential employees, conduct interviews, and perform background checks. When a new employee is hired, they welcome the person to the organization and give them an orientation. They often help administer employee benefits such as health insurance, retirement plans, and vacation days. They are typically tasked with processing payroll and help make sure the organization is in compliance with any local, state, or federal regulations. They also tend to be involved in employee relations, training, and annual review processes. In addition, HR specialists often oversee employees' satisfaction with their job and the workplace. They guide employees through all procedures and answer questions about policies. Above all, HR specialists serve as a link between the organization and the employee. Their general responsibility is to make sure that the organization finds, hires, retains, and develops the best employees it can.

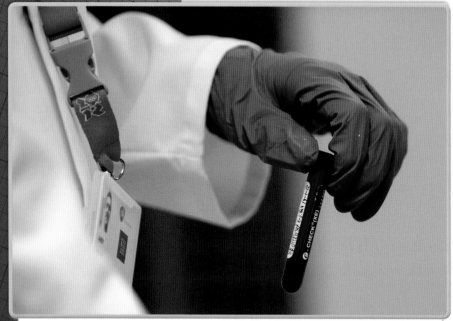

A scientist handles a vial of blood that will be tested as part of an antidoping program. Human resources personnel are responsible for reviewing drug testing rules with athletes and employees.

Bettina Davis is the vice president of human resources for Major League Baseball's Washington Nationals. She describes her role in an article for *HR Magazine,* saying, "I am manager, coach and trainer for people who support the team on the field. My challenge is to keep all of the players not on the field ready for the game." Some of the areas Davis focuses on at work include reviewing rules for testing players for drug use, staffing stadiums, and interpretation of labor laws and how it applies to a baseball team. Davis has also been invited to be on Major League Baseball's committee on diversity as an economic impact on the business. Even when the team is losing, Davis has a positive message for staff. "I tell staff, and job applicants, that if your expectation is to come to work where everything is done and you just continue to do what the previous person was doing, this isn't for you. If you want to be part of a legacy, be challenged every day and see the fruits of your labor, that's what you'll be doing here," she said in the article for *HR Magazine.*

HR: EDUCATIONAL AND PROFESSIONAL REQUIREMENTS

Most HR specialists have at least a bachelor's degree in human resources, business administration, sports management, or a related field. It is helpful to take courses in business, industrial relations, psychology, writing, HR management, and accounting. Some organizations require previous work experience, which can be gained by working as an HR assistant, doing customer service, or serving in a related job.

Some HR specialists who wish to advance to a higher level earn a master's degree in HR. They can specialize in areas such as HR management, organizational development, and HR performance. Some HR specialists chose to pursue a master's of business administration (MBA) in human resource management. Earning a graduate degree may help a person get promoted or land a better-paying, more senior position.

Although HR specialists don't need any certifications or licenses, some employers prefer or require it. HR professionals can earn certifications to show they are competent across all areas of human resources. Some certification programs include the Professional in Human Resources certification and the Senior Professional in Human Resources certification. To earn these, candidates must have worked a certain number of years in the field and pass a test.

HR: OPPORTUNITIES FOR ADVANCEMENT

HR specialists who work for large organizations that employ multiple levels and types of human resources professionals will have the best opportunity for advancement. Some advance to positions that have more responsibility and may supervise others. Some advance to even higher level positions, such as HR manager or director.

HR specialists are likely to be promoted if they demonstrate a thorough knowledge of their organization, its needs, and its regulatory requirements. Earning voluntary professional certifications or a master's degree in business administration or a related field can also improve a person's opportunities for advancement.

JOB OUTLOOK FOR HUMAN RESOURCES SPECIALISTS

According to the BLS's *Occupational Outlook Handbook*, HR specialist jobs are projected to increase. HR specialists who have general skills and are able to handle increasingly complex employment laws and health care options will be in demand.

At the same time, the increasing use of technology is expected to slow the rate of growth in this field. As more employers use the internet to recruit new employees and conduct other administrative tasks, they will need fewer HR employees to process employee records and information. Overall, though, job prospects for HR specialists are expected to be good. Candidates who have a bachelor's degree, voluntary certifications, and related work experience will have the best prospects for landing a job in the field.

SPORTS ACCOUNTANT

There's a lot of money in sports. From player salaries to television and sponsorship deals, the amounts can be staggering. Sports organizations need people with financial expertise to manage the money. Senior sports accountants or finance executives manage team finances. They oversee several employees and supervise the production of financial reports, budgets, and forecasts (predictions of what might happen regarding the business's financials). Using these reports and other data, finance executives use data analysis to find ways to reduce costs and increase profits. They may also make purchasing decisions, monitor revenue from ticket and concession sales, and be involved in the negotiation of player contracts. They also direct investment activities and help develop strategies to achieve the organization's long-term financial goals.

Finance executives often manage an accounting department. The accounting department of a sports franchise handles the day-to-day financial operations. Sports accountants oversee purchasing, sales, and accounts payable. For example, a Major League Baseball team may employ a senior accountant, a junior accountant, a staff accountant, a payroll accountant, and several assistants. Each accountant has specific responsibilities in the organization, such as monitoring revenue from ticket and concession sales, filing tax documents, paying accounts payable, collecting accounts receivable, and processing payroll. The accounting department also records each financial transaction to create detailed financial statements for financial managers and team executives.

Eric Blagg is the vice president of finance for the Greenville Drive in South Carolina, a minor league baseball team and Class A affiliate of the Boston Red Sox. During the winter and spring, he focuses on planning for the upcoming seasons, with days full of meetings and updating forecast schedules. In the summer, when the baseball season is in full swing, Blagg generates volumes of daily, weekly, and monthly financial reports for the team's management. After the season ends in the fall, Blagg's accounting department generates several reports that summarize the season's results. Then, they begin planning for the next year and creating a budget based on the current year's financial results. "One of the most challenging but also rewarding parts of the accountant's job in sports is to manage and provide actionable insight into the trends shown by the data we generate throughout the season. We process so many transactions in such a short period of time that we must make any changes needed very quickly in order to avoid missing a revenue opportunity that presents itself after the season starts," he said in an article on Accountemps.com.

SPORTS ACCOUNTANT: EDUCATIONAL AND PROFESSIONAL REQUIREMENTS

Most finance managers have at least a bachelor's degree in finance, accounting, economics, or business administration. Many employers prefer candidates who have a master's degree in business administration, finance, or economics. These programs teach students financial analysis and help them develop the analytical skills they will need for a career in finance.

Employers also prefer candidates who have work experience in a business or financial occupation. Finance managers can gain this experience by working as a loan officer, accountant, securities sales agent, or financial analyst.

Financial managers do not need to be certified to do their job. However, obtaining a certification can demonstrate competence and skill. Professional organizations

An accountant double-checks her figures before entering the numbers into a report that she is preparing for a management meeting.

such as the CFA Institute and the Association for Financial Professionals offer several certifications that can strengthen a candidate's résumé. The education, experience, and testing requirements vary for each certification.

Some financial managers who work as accountants choose to become certified public accountants (CPAs) or certified management accountants (CMAs). Investment professionals may choose to obtain the chartered financial analyst (CFA) certification, while those who work in treasury departments may choose to pursue a certified treasury professional credential.

Most financial professionals attend continuing education classes to keep up with the latest finance and accounting industry news. These classes help them understand changes in federal and state laws, new financial innovations, and global trade and accounting policies. Many organizations will pay for part or all of the cost of attending such classes.

SPORTS ACCOUNTANTS: OPPORTUNITIES FOR ADVANCEMENT

Sports accountants who work for larger organizations generally have more opportunities to advance to higher positions. They typically start in entry-level positions and move up to become managers, positions that have additional responsibility. Others advance to higher level positions, such as CFO, controller, or treasurer. "It's a great career path, but wanting to be a sports accountant isn't as simple as being an accountant who's a sports fan. You might have to be very flexible as to location and relocation to get a position in sports or to progress in a sports career due to the limited number of positions in each geographical market. Most sports organizations are minor league and have small accounting staffs of one or two individuals. Advancement within the profession would generally require moving to a pro-level organization where the accounting team is more robust," said Eric Blagg in the article for Accountemps.com.

Experienced sports accountants who demonstrate a thorough knowledge of their organization, its needs, and its regulatory requirements are more likely to be promoted. Professionals who earn certifications or a master's degree in business administration may be more likely to be considered for a promotion.

JOB OUTLOOK FOR SPORTS ACCOUNTANTS

According to the BLS's *Occupational Outlook Handbook*, finance manager jobs are projected to increase in the next decade. This rate of growth is about the same as the average growth rate for all occupations.

A group of business office professionals, including sports accountants, meet in a conference room to go over the latest team budget and forecast.

As the sports industry grows, accountants and finance managers will continue to be in demand. As organizations accumulate cash assets, they will need financial managers who have experience handling and investing cash to plan, direct, and coordinate investments. The increasing use of technology may have a negative effect on the number of jobs for financial staff, as fewer people will be needed to perform the same amount of work. However, this is expected to have a greater impact on lower-level finance staff, as technology will allow companies to use fewer people to manage and process financial transactions and records. The need for finance managers who can analyze data and recommend how to improve company profits is expected to continue, as this type of analysis is an important part of helping a company succeed.

Overall, sports accountants have good job prospects. Although competition for jobs will be intense, candidates who have experience in accounting and finance and have a master's degree or certification will have the best prospects.

WORKING CONDITIONS IN THE BUSINESS OFFICE

General counsel, HR specialists, and accountants generally spend most of their time working in an office. Some travel to attend job fairs, visit college campuses, or meet with job applicants. Most work full time or forty hours per week, typically during defined hours. Overtime may be

Toronto Blue Jays player Jose Reyes hits a home run during a game against the Baltimore Orioles. Many people work behind the scenes to run professional sports leagues like MLB.

required, especially when deadlines are upcoming. Some positions feature flexible hours and telecommuting.

SPORTS PERSONNEL CAREERS: A DREAM JOB

For many people, working in the sports industry can be like hitting a home run. Beyond the field, there are many lucrative opportunities for people to explore in sports personnel careers. From public relations to accounting, these careers keep the business of sports running smoothly so that fans worldwide can cheer on their favorite teams.

COLLEGE AND UNIVERSITY PROGRAMS IN SPORTS PERSONNEL

Endicott College
376 Hale Street
Beverly, MA 01915
(978) 232-2433
http://www.endicott.edu
Programs of study: Athletic training, sports management

SUNY College at Cortland
Studio West Building, Room 156F
PO Box 2000
Cortland, NY 13045
(607) 753-5537
http://www2.cortland
    .edu/departments
    /sport-management
Programs of study:
    Sports management,
    international sports
    management

Temple University
1810 N. 13th Street

Speakman Hall 111
Philadelphia, PA 19122
(215) 204-8701
http://www.sthm.temple
    .edu/degree/bs-sports
    -degree.html
Programs of study:
    Sports and recreation
    management

University of Florida
PO Box 118208
Gainesville, FL 32611
(352) 392-4042
http://trsm.hhp.ufl.edu
Programs of study: Sports
    management, tourism,
    recreation, and event
    management

University of Miami
School of Education
PO Box 248065
Coral Gables, FL 33124

(305) 284-3025

http://sites
.education.miami.edu
/sport-administration

Programs of study: Sports
administration

University of Michigan

401 Washtenaw Avenue

Ann Arbor, MI 48109

(734) 647-8989

http://www.kines.umich
.edu/academics
/undergraduate-pro-
grams
/sport-management

Programs of study: Sports
management

University of Minnesota

1900 University Avenue SE

220 Cooke Hall

Minneapolis, MN 55455

(612) 625-5300

http://www.cehd.umn.edu
/kin/current/undergrad
/smgt.html

Programs of study: Sports
management

University of North
Carolina

Campus Box 8605

Chapel Hill, NC 27599

(919) 962-2022

http://exss.unc.edu

Programs of study: Exercise
and sport science
(sport administration
concentration)

University of Tampa

401 W. Kennedy Boulevard

Tampa, FL 33606

(813) 257-3497

http://www.ut.edu

Programs of study: Sports
management

University of Texas

1 University Station

Austin, TX 78712

(512) 471-1273

https://education.utexas
.edu

Programs of study: Sports
management

PUBLIC RELATIONS SPECIALIST

ACADEMICS

Bachelor's degree

EXPERIENCE

Internship and volunteer opportunities with local sports
teams and organizations

CAREER PATHS

Public relations specialists can focus on media relations
Some PR specialists focus on event marketing
Community relations is also an option

RESPONSIBILITIES

Write press releases
Prepare information for the media

Write speeches

Arrange for media interviews

Create promotional campaigns

Use social media to promote an organization

TALENT EVALUATOR AND SCOUT

ACADEMICS

Bachelor's degree

EXPERIENCE

Internship and volunteer opportunities with local sports teams and organizations

CAREER PATHS

Some scouts identify and recruit college players

Some scouts work for professional sports teams

Scouts can also promote high school players in search of a scholarship

RESPONSIBILITIES

Identify prospective athletes

Attend games and watch film of the athletes' performance

Talk to athletes and coaches to see if they are a good fit for the organization

Prepare scouting reports

Attend scouting meetings

LEGAL COUNSEL

ACADEMICS

Bachelor's degree

Law degree

EXPERIENCE

Internship and volunteer opportunities with local sports teams and organizations

CAREER PATHS

Legal counsel can work for law firms representing sports organizations

In-house legal counsel work directly for an organization

Some legal counsel open their own practice

RESPONSIBILITIES

Review and negotiate all team contracts, media rights, and other deals

Negotiate and monitor contracts with corporate sponsors

Manage arena and stadiums legal needs

Manage seat-license sales

Prepare legal documents

HUMAN RESOURCES SPECIALIST

ACADEMICS

Bachelor's degree

EXPERIENCE

Internship and volunteer opportunities with local sports teams and organizations

CAREER PATHS

Human resources specialists work directly for a sports organization

Some HR specialists work for HR consulting companies

Some HR specialists open their own practice

RESPONSIBILITIES

Recruit and hire new employees

Conduct interviews

Oversee employee drug testing, background checks, credit checks, and other testing

Manage compensation and benefits

Give new employees orientations

Set up training sessions for employees

Manage employee assistance programs

Manage employee annual review process

SPORTS ACCOUNTANT

ACADEMICS

Bachelor's degree

EXPERIENCE

Internship and volunteer opportunities with local sports teams and organizations

CAREER PATHS

Sports accountants handle the recording of day-to-day financial transactions

Accountants can become finance managers.

Some accountants specialize in certain areas of finance.

RESPONSIBILITIES

Record financial transactions

Prepare financial statements

Perform analysis of financial statements

Prepare budgets and forecasts

Compare budgets and forecasts to actual results

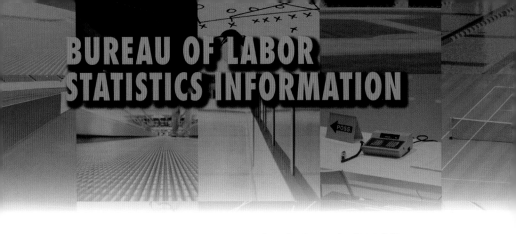

BUREAU OF LABOR
STATISTICS INFORMATION

PUBLIC RELATIONS SPECIALIST

What Public Relations Specialists Do—Public relations specialists create and maintain a favorable public image for the organization they represent. They design media releases to shape public perception of their organization and to increase awareness of its work and goals.

Work Environment—Public relations specialists usually work in offices. Some attend community activities. Long workdays are common, as is overtime.

How to Become a Public Relations Specialist—Public relations specialists typically need a bachelor's degree in public relations, journalism, communications, English, or business.

Job Outlook—Employment of public relations specialists is projected to grow 6 percent from 2014 to 2024, about as fast as the average for all occupations. The need for organizations to maintain their public image will continue to drive employment growth. Candidates can expect strong competition for jobs at advertising and public relations firms and organizations with large media exposure.

COACHES AND SCOUTS

What Coaches and Scouts Do—Coaches teach amateur or professional athletes the skills they need to succeed at their sport. Scouts look for new players and evaluate their skills and likelihood for success at the college, amateur, or professional level. Many coaches are also involved in scouting.

Work Environment—Coaches and scouts often work irregular hours, including evenings, weekends, and holidays. Full-time coaches usually work more than forty hours a week for several months during the sports season. Coaches travel frequently to sporting events. Scouts may be required to travel more extensively when searching for talented athletes.

How to Become a Coach or Scout—Coaches and scouts typically need a bachelor's degree. They must also have extensive knowledge of the game. Coaches typically gain this knowledge through their own experiences playing the sport at some level. Although previous playing experience may be beneficial, it is typically not required for most scouting jobs.

Job Outlook—Employment of coaches and scouts is projected to grow 6 percent from 2014 to 2024, about as fast as the average for all occupations. Increasing participation in high school and college sports will boost demand for coaches and scouts.

LAWYERS/GENERAL COUNSEL

What Lawyers Do—Lawyers advise and represent individuals, businesses, and government agencies on legal issues and disputes.

Work Environment—The majority of lawyers work in private and corporate legal offices. Some work for federal, local, and state governments. The majority work full-time, and many work more than forty hours a week.

How to Become a Lawyer—All lawyers must have a law degree and must also typically pass a state's written bar examination.

Job Outlook—Employment of lawyers is projected to grow 6 percent from 2014 to 2024, about as fast as the average for all occupations. Competition for jobs should continue to be strong because more students graduate from law school each year than there are jobs available.

HUMAN RESOURCES SPECIALISTS

What Human Resources Specialists Do—Human resources specialists recruit, screen, interview, and place workers. They often handle other human resources work, such as those related to employee relations, compensation and benefits, and training.

Work Environment—Human resources specialists generally work in offices. Some, particularly recruitment specialists, travel extensively to attend job fairs, visit college campuses, and meet with applicants. Most human resources specialists work full time during regular business hours.

How to Become a Human Resources Specialist—Applicants must usually have a bachelor's degree in human resources, business, or a related field. However, the level of education and experience required varies by position and employer.

Job Outlook—Employment of human resources specialists is projected to grow 5 percent from 2014 to 2024, about as fast as the average for all occupations. Human resources specialists will be needed to handle increasingly complex employment laws and health care coverage options. Most growth is projected to be in the employment services industry.

FINANCIAL MANAGER

What Financial Managers Do—Financial managers are responsible for the financial health of an organization. They produce financial reports, direct investment activities, and develop strategies and plans for the long-term financial goals of their organization.

Work Environment—Financial managers work in

many industries, including banks and insurance companies. Most financial managers work full time, and about one in three worked more than forty hours per week in 2014.

How to Become a Financial Manager—Financial managers typically have a bachelor's degree and five years or more of experience in another business or financial occupation, such as an accountant, auditor, securities sales agent, or financial analyst.

Job Outlook—Employment of financial managers is projected to grow 7 percent from 2014 to 2024, about as fast as the average for all occupations. As with other managerial occupations, job seekers are likely to face competition because there are more applicants than job openings. Candidates with a master's degree or certification should enjoy the best job prospects.

GLOSSARY

accredited Officially recognized or authorized.

aptitude An ability to do something.

budget An estimate of income and expenses for a period of time.

compensation The money received as salary or wages.

dolly A low truck or cart with small wheels for moving loads too heavy to be carried by hand.

facility A place for a specific purpose, such as a stadium or an arena.

forecast To predict or estimate a future event or trend.

internship A temporary job training position that may be paid or unpaid.

job shadowing An experience in which a student learns about a job by following around a worker in that field.

jurisdiction The power or right to exercise legal authority over a person, subject matter, or territory.

logo A symbol that represents an organization and/or its products.

marketing The act of promoting a business and its products or services.

media rights The exclusive right to broadcast a sporting event live.

merchandising Promoting the sale of goods.

press release An official statement to the media about a particular matter.

profile A written document that describes a player and his or her athletic qualities and character.

promotion A publicity campaign for a particular product, service, or company.

revenue A company's income.

sponsorship Providing financial support to a team or organization.

venue A place where a sporting event happens, such as a stadium or arena.

FOR MORE INFORMATION

Association for Financial Professionals (AFP)

4520 East West Highway, Suite 800
Bethesda, MD 20814

(301) 907-2862

Website: http://www.afponline.org

Facebook: @afpsocial

Twitter: @afponline

The AFP is the professional society that represents finance executives globally.

College Sports Information Directors of America (CoSIDA)

PO Box 7818

Greenwood, IN 46142-6427

Website: http://www.cosida.com

Facebook: @aaacosida

Twitter: @CoSIDAnews

This organization has members working in college sports public relations, media relations, and communications/information in the United States and Canada. It provides members with professional development and continuing education.

International Facility Management Association (IFMA)

800 Gessner Road, Suite 900

Houston, TX 77024-4257

(713) 623-4362

Website: http://www.ifma.org

Facebook: @InternationalFacilityManagementAssociation

Twitter: @IFMA

The IFMA is the world's largest and most widely recognized international association for facility management professionals. It sponsors industry conferences and publishes materials for people working in facilities management.

National Association of Collegiate Directors of Athletics (NACDA)

24651 Detroit Road

Westlake, OH 44145

(440) 892-4000

Website: http://www.nacda.com

Facebook: @NACDA

Twitter: @NACDA

NACDA is the largest association of collegiate athletics administrators, with members from the United States, Canada, and Mexico. It provides opportunities for networking, exchange of information and ideas, and training.

North American Society for Sport Management (NASSM)

135 Winterwood Drive

Butler, PA 16001

(724) 482-6277

Website: http://www.nassm.com

Twitter: @nassm_sportmgt

NASSM is an organization of professionals and students in
the fields of sport, leisure, and recreation, with members across North America, including the United States
and Canada.

Society for Human Resource Management

1800 Duke Street #100

Alexandria, VA 22314

(800) 283-7476

Website: https://www.shrm.org

Facebook: @societyforhumanresourcemanagement

Twitter: @SHRM

The world's largest society for HR professionals offers information and tools about a variety of HR topics, including
certification, training, and career tracks.

Sponsorship Marketing Council Canada

150 Eglinton Avenue East, Suite 402

Toronto, ON M4P 1E8

Canada

(647) 748-3615

Website: http://www.sponsorshipmarketing.ca/contact.html

Twitter: @SMCC_CCC

This organization's goal is to help brand marketers,
agency partners, and sponsorship sales teams work

together to promote sponsorship marketing with educational programs, collaboration, and sharing industry best practices.

Sport Marketing Association (SMA)

1972 Clark Avenue

Alliance, OH, 44601

(330) 829-8207

Website: http://www.sportmarketingassociation.com

Facebook: @SportMarketingAssociation

The SMA promotes professional interaction among professionals, teachers, and professors, and students worldwide to share knowledge in sport marketing.

WEBSITES

Because of the changing nature of internet links, Rosen Publishing has developed an online list of websites related to the subject of this book. This site is updated regularly. Please use this link to access the list:

http://www.rosenlinks.com/GCSI/Personnel

FOR FURTHER READING

Bodet, Gib. *Gib Bodet, Major League Scout: Twelve Thousand Baseball Games and Six Million Miles.* Jefferson, NC: McFarland & Co., 2014.

Buckley, James. *Sports Media Relations.* Broomall, PA: Mason Crest, 2016.

Burgan, Michael. *Working in College Sports.* Broomall, PA: Mason Crest, 2016.

Calvin, Michael. *The Nowhere Men: The Unknown Story of Football's True Talent Spotters.* London, UK: Random House UK, 2013.

Edelman, Marc, and Geoffrey Christopher Rapp. *Careers in Sports Law.* Chicago, IL: American Bar Association, Forum on the Entertainment and Sports Industries, 2014.

Freedman, Jeri. *Dream Jobs in Sports Management and Administration.* New York, NY: Rosen Publishing, 2013.

Furgang, Kathy. *Dream Jobs in Sports Law.* New York, NY: Rosen Publishing, 2015.

Furgang, Kathy. *Dream Jobs in Stadium and Sports Facility Operations.* New York, NY: Rosen Publishing, 2014.

Genovese, George. *A Scout's Report: My 70 Years in Baseball.* Jefferson, NC: McFarland & Co., 2015.

Gigliotti, Jim. *Sports Arena & Event Management.* Broomall, PA: Mason Crest, 2016.

Gitlin, Marty. *Dream Jobs in Sports Finance and*

Administration. New York, NY: Rosen Publishing, 2015.

Gitlin, Marty. *Dream Jobs in Sports Scouting.* New York, NY: Rosen Publishing, 2014.

Mattern, Joanne. *So, You Want to Work in Sports? The Ultimate Guide to Exploring the Sports Industry.* New York, NY: Aladdin, 2014.

Mitchell, Lincoln Abraham. *Will Big League Baseball Survive? Globalization, the End of Television, Youth Sports, and the Future of Major League Baseball.* Philadelphia, PA: Temple University Press, 2017.

Mullin, Bernard, Stephen Hardy, and William Sutton. *Sport Marketing.* 4th ed. Champlain, IL: Human Kinetics, 2014.

Niver, Heather Moore. *Dream Jobs in Sports Marketing.* New York, NY: Rosen Publishing, 2012.

Schmidt, Debra. *Careers in Sports and Fitness.* San Diego, CA: ReferencePoint, 2016.

Schwartz, Eric C., et al. *Managing Sport Facilities and Major Events.* London, UK: Routledge, 2017.

Trask, Amy. *You Negotiate Like a Girl: Reflections on a Career in the National Football League.* Chicago, IL: Triumph, 2016.

Wong, Glenn M. *The Comprehensive Guide to Careers in Sports.* Burlington, MA: Jones & Bartlett Learning, 2013.

BIBLIOGRAPHY

Accountemps. "What's the Score? A Peek Inside Sports Accounting Jobs." March 4, 2015. https://www .roberthalf.com/accountemps/blog/whats-the-score -a-peek-inside-sports-accounting-jobs.

Betzer, Jason. "Sports Management 101: Breaking Into the Business of Sports." Forbes.com, February 5, 2014. http://www.forbes.com/sites/jasonbel-zer/2014/02/05 /sports-industry-101-breaking-into-the-business-of -sports/#11417af13db9.

Betzer, Jason. "Want a Job in the Sports Industry? Good News, Because It's an Employee's Market." Forbes. com, December 17, 2015. http://www.forbes.com/ sites/jasonbelzer/2015/12/17/want-a-job-in-the -sports-industry-good-news-because-its-an -employees-market/#58fd30943cd2.

Boutselis, Pamme. "Get in the Game with a Degree in Sport Management." Southern New Hampshire University, November 19, 2015. http://www.snhu.edu /about-us/news-and-events/2015/11/get-in-the -game-with-a-degree-in-sport-management.

Clapp, Brian. "How 10 MLB General Managers Began Their Sports Careers." WorkInSports.com, March 30, 2015. http://www.workinsports.com/blog/how-ten-mlb-general-managers-began-their-sports-careers.

Clapp, Brian. "How to Get a Job in Community Relations with a Professional Sports Team." WorkInSports .com. March 15, 2015. http://www.workinsports.com

/blog/sports-jobs-community-relations-jobs.

Clapp, Brian. "Inside the World of Corporate Sponsorship in Sports." WorkInSports.com, January 11, 2016. http://www.workinsports.com/blog /inside-the-world-of-corporate-sponsorship-in -sports.

Clapp, Brian. "Starting a Career in Media Sports Relations." WorkInSports.com, November 23, 2015. http://www.workinsports.com/blog /starting-a-career-in-sports-media-relations.

Clapp, Brian. "Why a Sports Management Degree Will Separate You from the Competition." WorkInSports .com, November 16, 2015. http://www.workinsports. com/blog/why-a-sports-management-degree-will -separate-you-from-the-competition.

Denholm, Kristin Meldrum. "Turning Your Love of Sports into a College Major and a Career." *USA Today*, December 30, 2015. http://usatodayhss .com/2015/turning-your-love-of-sports-into-a -college-major-and-a-career.

Dosh, Kristi, "Seek Out Opportunities in Sports." KristiDosh.com, March 8, 2013. http://www.kristi-dosh.com/2013/03/08 /seek-out-opportunities-in-sports.

Dyer, Kristian. "Following the Life of a Scout as NFL Draft Approaches." Metro, October 10, 2014. http:// www.metro.us/sports/following -the-life-of-a-scout-as-nfl-draft-approaches /tmWnef---24iPOO5ta7ogs.

Farmer, Sam. "Falcons GM Thomas Dimitroff Has Risen from a Humble Football Beginning to Potential Super Bowl Winner." *Los Angeles Times*, January 30, 2017. http://www.latimes.com/sports/nfl

/la-sp-patriots-falcons-dimitroff-20170130-story
.html.

The Fields of Green. "FOG Roundtable: The Media
Coverage of Sports Business, Part 2." October 16,
2014. http://thefieldsofgreen.com/2014/10/16
/fog-roundtable-the-media-coverage-of-sports
-business-part-two.

Forgotten Harvest. "The Detroit Pistons Celebrate
Thanksgiving with Metro Detroit Families."
November 2016. http://www.forgottenharvest.org
/page.aspx?p=132.

Garcia, Ahiza. "NBA Becomes First Major US Sports
League to Allow Ads on Jerseys." CNN.com, April 15,
2016. http://money.cnn.com/2016/04/15/news
/nba-jerseys-corporate-sponsors.

Kryk, John. "Ontario-Raised Thomas Dimitroff's Rise to
Falcons GM." *Toronto Sun*, February 2, 2017. www.
torontosun.com/2017/02/02
/ontario-raised-thomas-dimitroffs-rise-to-falcons
-gm-began-humbly-as-cfl-scout.

Langhorst, Paul. "5 Key Benefits of Becoming a Youth
Sports Referee/Umpire." Engage Sports, December 9,
2015. http://www.engagesports.com/blog
/post/431/5-key-benefits-of-becoming-a-youth
-sports-referee-umpire.

Martin, Natalie. "Alumni Spotlight: Emmy Latham."
Julian Krinsky Camps & Programs, January 31, 2017.
https://info.jkcp.com/blog
/alumni-spotlight-emmy-latham.

NC State University. "Sport Management Degree Takes
Young Alumna to the Super Bowl." February 10, 2017.
https://cnr.ncsu.edu/news/2017/02
/sport-management-degree-to-super-bowl.

O'Neill, Dana. "The Tales of a College Basketball Student Manager." ESPN.com, July 9, 2015. http://www.espn .com/mens-college-basketball/story/_/id/13215054 /the-life-college-basketball-student-manager.

Simmons, Steve. "Blue Jays GM Alex Anthopoulos: A Day in the Life." *Toronto Sun*, February 28, 2013. http://www.torontosun.com/2013/02/28/a-day-in -the-life-of-blue-jays-gm-alex-anthopoulos.

Spanberg, Erik. "Teams Find Safety in Numbers When It Comes to Their Legal Staff." *Sports Business Journal*, May 11, 2015. http://m.sportsbusinessdaily.com /Journal/Issues/2015/05/11/In-Depth/Team-counsel .aspx?.

Zeidner, Rita. "Inside Baseball." *HR Magazine*, May 1, 2010. http://www.shrm.org/hr-today/news/hr -magazine/pages/0510ziedner.aspx.

Zimmerman, Lisa. "Do You Have What It Takes to Be an NFL Scout?" NFL Player Engagement. http://www .nflplayerengagement.com/life/articles/nfl-scout.

INDEX

ABOUT THE AUTHOR

Carla Mooney is a graduate of the University of Pennsylvania. She writes for young people and is the author of numerous educational books. She is an avid sports fan and enjoys watching football, hockey, baseball, and the Olympics!

PHOTO CREDITS

Design: Brian Garvey; Layout: Ellina Litmanovich; Editor: Bethany Bryan; Photo Researcher: Sherri Jackson